3

THIS WALKER BOOK BELONGS TO:

_____

_____

_____

LEMON SHARK
3.3 metres

SAND TIGER SHARK
3 metres

PORT JACKSON SHARK
1.2 metres

NURSE SHARK
3 metres

GOBLIN SHARK
3.3 metres

SWELL SHARK
1 metre

DWARF LANTERN
SHARK
0.17 metres

BULL SHARK
3.2 metres

WHALE SHARK
12 metres

COOKIE-CUTTER SHARK
0.4 metres

ZEBRA SHARK
2.5 metres

TIGER SHARK
5 metres

For the children of Hudson Primary
School, Sunderland – N.D.

For Mum, Dad, Lisa
and Wayne
– J.C.

First published 2003 by Walker Books Ltd
87 Vauxhall Walk, London SE11 5HJ

This edition published 2004

1 2 3 4 5 6 7 8 9 10

Text © 2003 Nicola Davies
Illustrations © 2003 James Croft

The right of Nicola Davies and James Croft to be identified as author
and illustrator respectively of this work has been asserted by them
in accordance with the Copyright, Designs and Patents Act 1988

This book has been typeset in Blockhead and Sitcom

Printed in China

British Library Cataloguing in Publication Data:
a catalogue record for this book
is available from the British Library

ISBN 1-84428-458-1

www.walkerbooks.co.uk

SURPRISING
SHARKS

Nicola Davies

illustrated by
James Croft

WALKER BOOKS
AND SUBSIDIARIES
LONDON · BOSTON · SYDNEY · AUCKLAND

Wait for me!

You're swimming in the warm blue sea.
What's the one word that turns your
dream into a nightmare?
What's the one word that
makes you think of
a giant
man-eating
killer?

Shark? Yes, it is a shark!

It's a **DWARF LANTERN SHARK**.
The smallest kind of shark in the world, it is
just bigger than a chocolate bar. Not a giant,
certainly no man-eater and only a killer
if you happen to be a shrimp.

9

You see, MOST sharks are not at all what you might expect. After all, who would expect a shark to ...

Like all **LANTERN SHARKS** this **BLACKBELLY LANTERN SHARK** can make light shine from its tummy. This helps it to blend in with the silvery surface of the sea and avoid ending up as dinner for bigger fish.

have built-in fairy lights ...

or blow up like a party balloon ...

SWELL SHARKS swallow water when they get scared and blow up to three times their normal size so that they can wedge themselves between rocks and no predator can pull them out.

This Australian shark is called a **WOBBEGONG**. Its patterned skin matches the rocks and corals on the sea floor, so it can sneak up on shellfish, crabs and small fish unseen.

lie on the sea floor like a scrap of old carpet...

Look out!

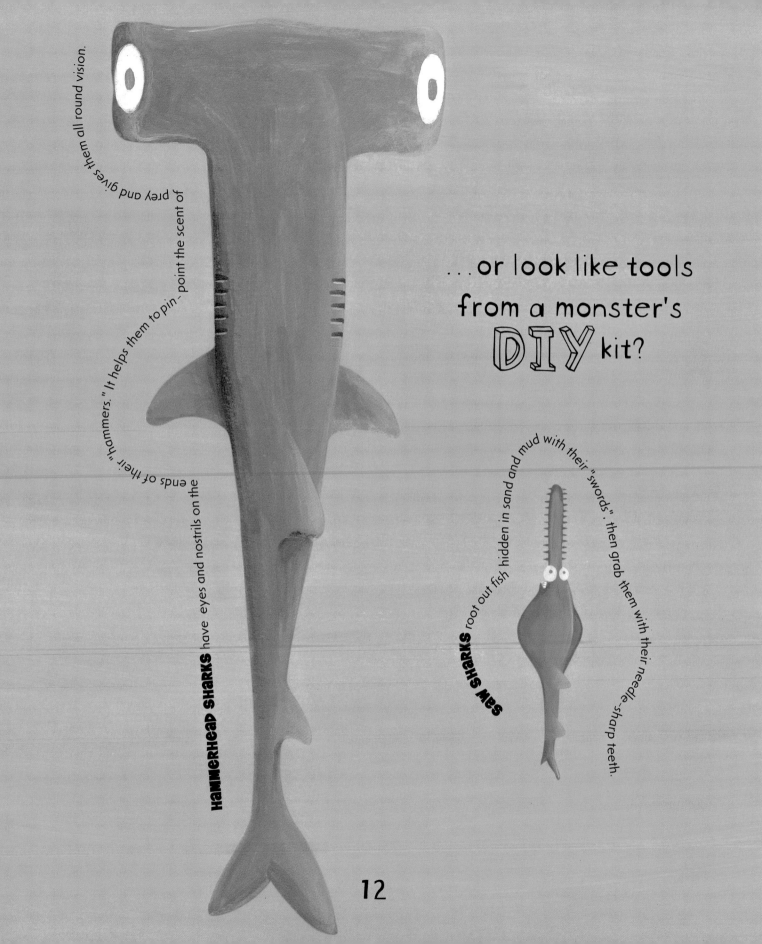

...or look like tools from a monster's **DIY** kit?

HAMMERHEAD SHARKS have eyes and nostrils on the ends of their "hammers." It helps them to pin-point the scent of prey and gives them all round vision.

SAW SHARKS root out fish hidden in sand and mud with their "swords", then grab them with their needle-sharp teeth.

12

In fact, sharks come in all sorts of shapes and sizes.

BLUE SHARK

COOKIE-CUTTER SHARK

NURSE SHARK

ANGEL SHARK

GOBLIN SHARK

How can such different animals all be sharks?
Look carefully and you'll see
all the things they share.

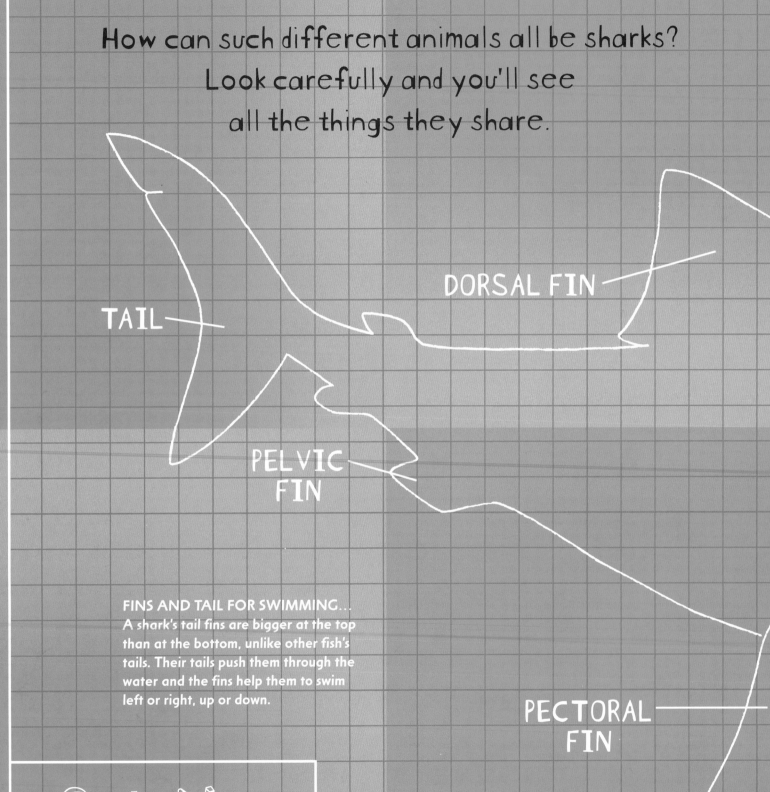

TAIL

DORSAL FIN

PELVIC
FIN

FINS AND TAIL FOR SWIMMING...
A shark's tail fins are bigger at the top
than at the bottom, unlike other fish's
tails. Their tails push them through the
water and the fins help them to swim
left or right, up or down.

PECTORAL
FIN

Outside:

14

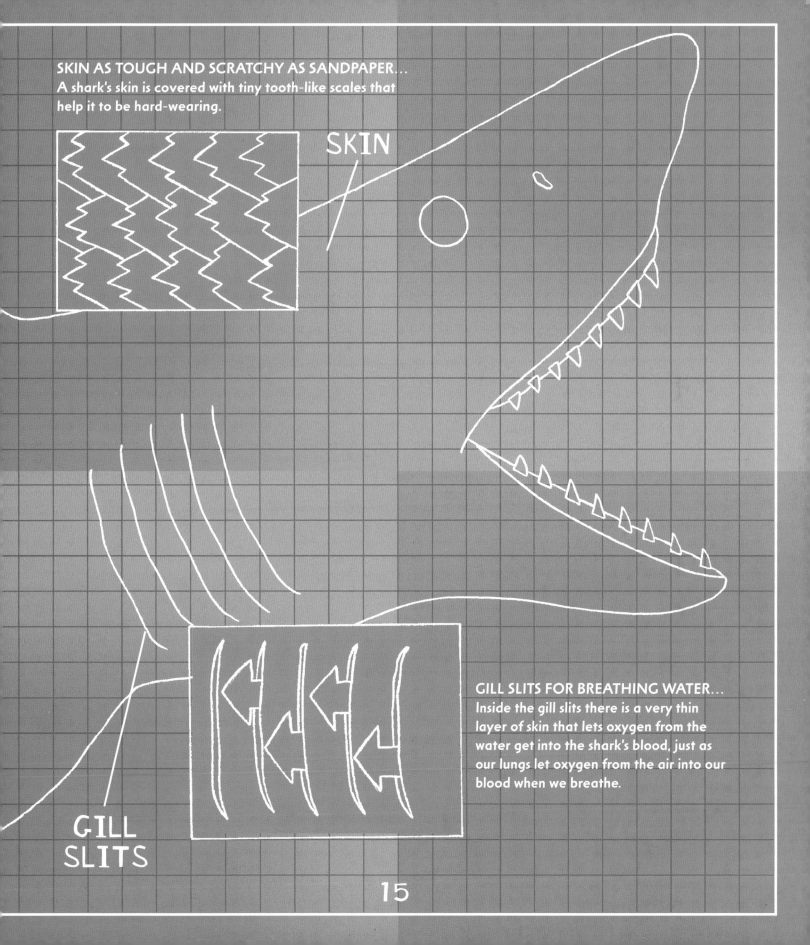

SKIN AS TOUGH AND SCRATCHY AS SANDPAPER...
A shark's skin is covered with tiny tooth-like scales that help it to be hard-wearing.

SKIN

GILL SLITS FOR BREATHING WATER...
Inside the gill slits there is a very thin layer of skin that lets oxygen from the water get into the shark's blood, just as our lungs let oxygen from the air into our blood when we breathe.

GILL SLITS

Inside:

JAWS THAT CAN POP OUT THROUGH
THE MOUTH, LIKE A JACK-IN-THE-BOX...
Sharks' jaws aren't part of their heads like
ours are. Instead they're held on by a kind of
living rubber band, so the jaws can shoot
forward fast to grab prey.

JAWS

TEETH

ROWS AND ROWS OF SPARE TEETH, SO
THAT THE SHARK IS NEVER WITHOUT ITS BITE...
A shark can have up to 3,000 teeth, all in rows
one behind the other. As one tooth wears out,
the one behind moves forward to replace it.
So sharks always have sharp teeth and use
more than 20,000 in their lifetime.

A BENDY, BONELESS SKELETON THAT
HELPS STOP IT SINKING…
Sharks' skeletons are made of a tough kind of
the stuff called cartilage – the same thing that
your ears and the end of your nose are made
of. Cartilage floats in water like a rubber ball.

SKELETON

But it isn't the basic body plan
that makes sharks sharks …

it's the **sharkish** way they behave!
Sharks are always hungry and they're
always on the lookout for their next meal.
Some even start **killing**
before they're born.

SAND TIGER SHARKS
give birth to just two
live young – which is all
that's left after those two
have eaten the other six
babies in their mother's belly.

Let's get him!

Some sharks lay eggs and some give birth to live
young. But all baby sharks are just like their
parents, with **sharp teeth** and
the ability to hunt right from the start.

DOGFISH lay eggs called "mermaids' purses", which have strings that tangle in the weeds to keep them safe in storms.

PORT JACKSON SHARKS lay eggs like a corkscrew, which sticks fast in rock crevices.

Sharks' senses are fine-tuned, ready for the tiniest hint that might mean food!

Sharks have tiny holes to let sound into their inner ears. They can hear sounds that are too low for our ears to pick up.

Sharks' eyes are on the sides of their heads, so they can see almost as well behind them as they can in front!

The whole of a shark's skin is sensitive in the same way that your fingertips are. You can tell hot from cold, rough from smooth, moving from still. A shark can also get all sorts of information from the movement and temperature of the water all around its body.

To a hungry shark, the faintest trail of clues is as clear as a restaurant sign.

A shark's nostrils are just under the tip of the snout. Water flows into them as the shark moves forward, bringing any scents with it.

Gel-filled pits in a shark's nose can detect food. Every animal has nerves, which are like cables carrying electrical messages around the body. The shark's gel pits can sense this electricity.

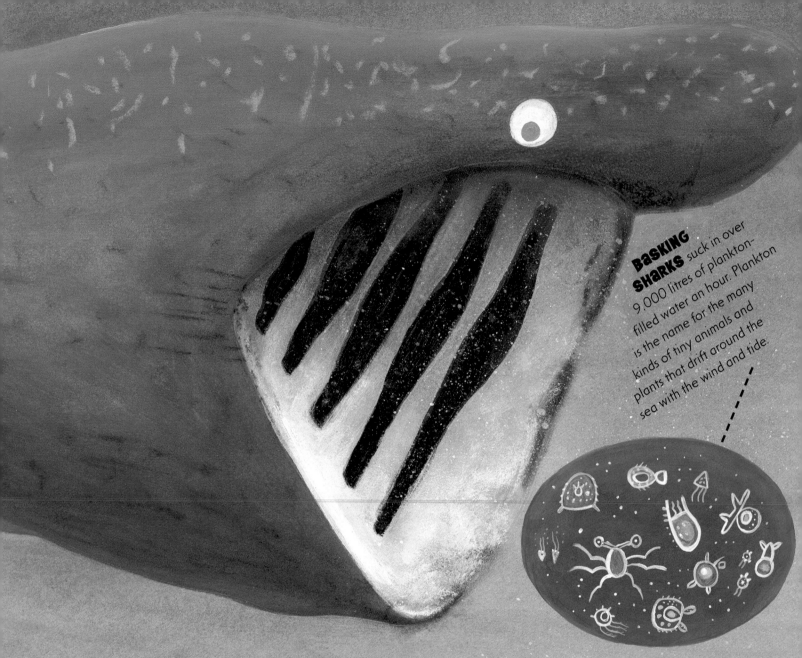

BASKING SHARKS suck in over 9,000 litres of plankton-filled water an hour. Plankton is the name for the many kinds of tiny animals and plants that drift around the sea with the wind and tide.

And when at last they're close enough for the kill, they feel the ᴄʀᴀᴄᴋʟᴇ of their prey's living nerves, so they bite in just the right place ... no matter what the prey! Whether it's **plankton** ...

or **people!** Oh yes, it's true – some sharks do kill people; about six of us every year.

The **GREAT WHITE** is one of just three species of shark that attack people regularly. The other two are the **BULL SHARK** and the **TIGER SHARK**. In fact, only 30 of the 500 different kinds of shark have ever attacked humans. Crocodiles, elephants, dogs and even pigs kill more people every year than sharks do!

But every year **people** kill **100 million** sharks.

Shark-tooth necklace

Machine grease

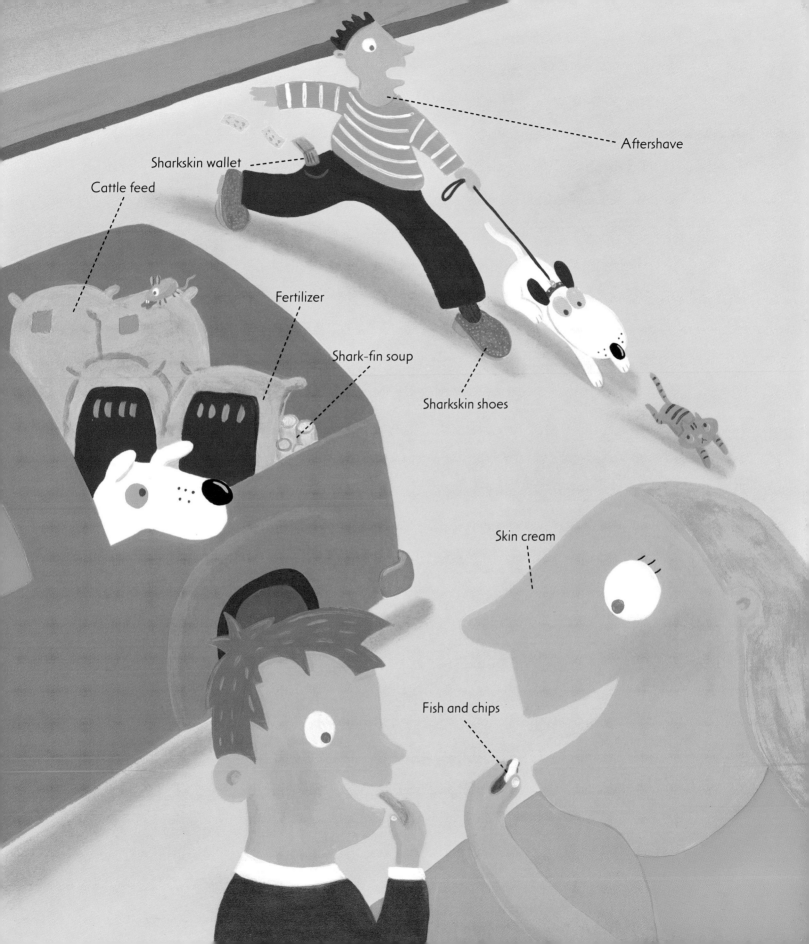

him. As he struggled for breath on the floor, Sita laughed at him, which made him very angry. When many attendants had moved the bow to one side, Ravana went back to his seat, quite humiliated. Finally Rama came forward, lifted the bow easily and, as he tried to bend it, it broke in two. The assembled crowds rose to their feet as King Janaka declared Rama the winner of the contest. A few days later Rama and Sita were married.'

Ravana, his son and his brother are killed in battle:

'Rama collected an army of monkeys with the help of his friend King Sugriva and Sugriva's general Hanuman, and attacked Lanka. Many battles took place. In one battle, Lakshmana was badly injured, but the doctor cured him using medicinal herbs. In the final battle Ravana, his son and his brother were killed by Rama. Sita was rescued from her captivity. After Ravana's youngest brother was declared King of Lanka, Rama, Sita and Lakshmana returned to Ayodhya with Hanuman.'

The final destruction of Ravana, his son and his brother is acted out on the **Dasara** day, when their effigies, filled with fireworks, are set alight.

FOR DISCUSSION

1 What are the moral teachings of the stories?

2 How are they put across? Why might this way be more effective than others that might be used?

THINGS TO DO

1 Draw a cartoon of one part of the story of Rama and Sita.

Effigies of Ravana, his son and his brother.

16 **The scriptures and Hindu weddings**

This unit tells you how the Hindu scriptures are used in weddings.

A Hindu wedding ceremony is based on the Ashwalayana Grihya Sutra text, which gives the rules of procedure, the correct order of rituals and the Sanskrit mantra for each ritual. In some regions of India the order of rituals is changed; this does not affect the ceremony. However, if two separate rituals are combined to produce a new ritual not mentioned in the scripture, a part of the ceremony becomes incorrect and creates confusion.

A personal experience

Here is how one Hindu describes what happened at a wedding in Britain:
'Anil and Anita are British-born Hindus and English is their first language. They do not know Sanskrit, but they wanted a full ceremony with the Sanskrit mantras from the scriptures. They repeated the mantras after

A bride and bridegroom walk the seven steps.

the priest to make their responses as he led them through ten parts of the ceremony, keeping carefully to the correct order.

1 Anita's parents offered puja to their family deities and God Ganesha.
2 Anil's family were received by Anita's parents at the door of the hall. Anil was given a little honey in welcome. At each ritual in the ceremony the priest chanted the appropriate mantra from the scriptures.
3 Anita was formally given in marriage. Anil promised Anita that he would be moderate in the practice of his dharma, **artha** and **kama**.
4 Verses of blessing were sung and the couple were showered with rice grains at the end of each verse.
5 The couple garlanded each other and showered each other with rice. Each tied a piece of soft cotton thread around the other's wrist. Anil then gave Anita her wedding necklace of black beads.
6 Anil took Anita's right hand and said the following mantra in Sanskrit:

'I take your hand, my bride, for good luck. May we grow old together. The Gods Bhaga, Aryaman, Surya and Indra have entrusted you to me as my life partner.'
(Rig-Veda 10. 85. 36.)

7 The marriage **homa** was performed. The couple made offerings of wood, ghee, grain and roasted millet to Agni (God of Fire) and walked around it in reverence, praying for children, health and long married life.
8 Then came the saptapadi ritual. Anil and Anita walked seven steps together in a line near the holy fire as the scriptures demanded. For each step Anil spoke the Sanskrit mantra:

'My bride, follow me in my vows. Take the first step for food...take the second step for strength...the third for increasing prosperity...the fourth for happiness...the fifth for children. May we have many healthy and long-lived sons. Take the sixth step for seasonal pleasures...take the seventh step for lifelong friendship.'
(Ashwalayana Grihya Sutra.)

9 The priest and senior members of both families blessed the couple.
10 That night Anil and Anita looked up at the Pole Star, promising to be constant to each other.

NEW WORDS

Artha, kama the bridegroom promises that he will be moderate in the practice of his dharma (religious and social duties), artha (earning money) and kama (enjoying the good things of life)

Homa a ritual in which offerings of wood, ghee and grain are made to Agni (God of Fire)

FOR DISCUSSION

1 What did Anil mean when he promised moderation in all things?
2 What is moderation in dharma, artha and kama?
3 How is God present in a Hindu wedding?
4 Why are Hindu marriages (like all marriages in India, including Christian ones) usually arranged by parents and/or other relatives?

THINGS TO DO

1 Make a collage of a scene from a Hindu wedding, or show a wedding in the form of a strip cartoon (decide how many scenes you will include).
2 List the symbolic actions in the wedding ceremony and write down their meanings.

This unit is about the use of scriptures in two separate religious rituals, performed when a baby is born, and when it is given a name.

Children are warmly welcomed in Hindu families. Their safe arrival is prayed for, and their welcome and caring entry to the family group are made clear by the many rituals found in the ancient scriptures which focus on a new baby's well-being.

A baby is born

The Grihya Sutra text by Ashwalayana says:

'When a baby is born its father should come to see it. He should bathe and put on clean clothes. Afterwards he offers prayers to God. Gently holding the baby in his lap, he should turn to the east and, using a gold ring, put a few drops of honey and ghee mixture in the baby's mouth. Then he should say: "Dear child, I give you this honey and ghee which is provided by God, who is the Creator of the world. May you be protected by God and live in this world for a hundred autumns. By God's grace may you become strong and firm like a rock, an axe for the wicked, and bright in character. May God give you long life and understanding of the Vedas."'

This ritual is performed mainly in devout Brahmin families. In the past, when most babies were born at home, the ritual could be done soon after birth. But today, in large cities, many babies are born in hospitals, so this ritual is performed as soon as the mother and child return home.

The naming of a child

With the giving of a name, the child becomes an individual personality in the family.

The Ashwalayana Grihya Sutra says:

'This sacrament of naming a baby should be performed on the 11th or 12th day after birth. The father should worship the family gods and goddesses before noon, with the help of the family priest. Rice grains should be spread on a metal plate and, using a gold ring, the chosen name should be written in the rice. Prayers are said so that the baby will be clever and healthy and grow up to be dutiful.'

A father and child after the naming ceremony.

The text recommends that:

'The name of a boy should be pleasing in sound and easy to say. Girls should be named after stars, such as Rohini, or after rivers, such as Ganga or Kaveri, or after birds, like the Maina.'

This religious ritual is performed mainly in devout Brahmin families, but many Hindus celebrate the occasion in the afternoon on the twelfth day by inviting relatives and friends. The baby is dressed in new clothes and placed in a cradle. Some families light twelve lamps and place them under the cradle. The chosen name of the baby is announced by the eldest woman in the family. Invited women with children sing cradle songs in which the baby's name is mentioned at the appropriate place. All guests then enjoy refreshments with special sweet dishes, prepared for the occasion.

In Britain, the naming of a baby is celebrated in many Hindu homes.

FOR DISCUSSION

1 Discuss the similarities and differences between the birth of a Hindu baby and one in your family. (If you are a Hindu was it exactly the same?)

THINGS TO DO

1 List the symbolic acts linked with a child's birth and write down their meanings.

2 Names have meanings. Find out what your name means and why you were given it (or them, if you have more than one).

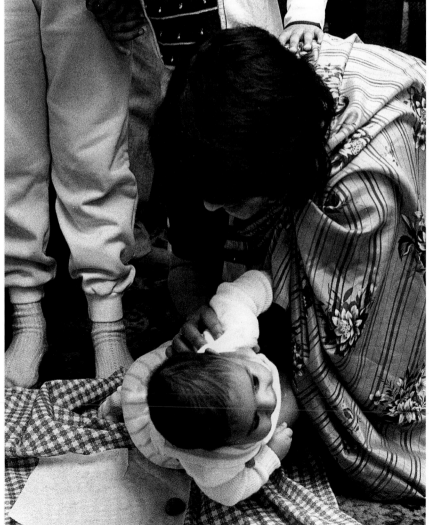

The naming of a Hindu baby.

18 Scriptures in the lives of children (2)

This unit tells you how a baby's first outing, its first haircut and the custom of ear-piercing are based on scriptures.

Traditionally, Hindu babies do not have to face the outside world until they are thought to be strong and healthy enough to do so.

A baby's first outing
The Ashwalayana Grihya Sutra says:

> 'The first outing may take place in the third or fourth month after birth. It should be done on a day when the moon will be clearly visible after dark, as the baby is taken to see it. The parents and the baby should bathe and wear new clothes, then the baby's father should offer morning worship to the family gods. Afterwards the parents should take the child out of the house to show the little one the sun for a few seconds.'

This ritual is designed to make the child aware of the world outside. Many Hindus take their children to the local temple for their first outing so that they may receive God's blessing. A four-month-old baby is made aware of light, darkness, different colours and shapes through this ritual.

The piercing of ear lobes
The surgeon Sushruta claims in his Sutra text (350CE) that:

> 'Ear-piercing is to be done for two reasons. Firstly, it will enable the child to wear earrings. Secondly, it will make a child healthy, long-lived and well-to-do.'

A young woman wearing earings and a nose stud.

This sacrament has been faithfully followed by Hindus in order to make certain of these blessings.

Many Hindu children have their ear lobes pierced on the afternoon of the naming day by the local goldsmith. Both boys and girls have their ear lobes pierced when they are a few months old if the ritual is not carried out on the naming day. Girls have their left nostrils pierced, too, at the age of four or five years, so that they can wear nose ornaments.

In India older married women often wear an expensive nose ring made of pearls bound into an attractive design by gold wire.

A child's first haircut

The Sanskrit name for the first haircut is **Chaulam**. The Grihya Sutra of Paraskara says that this sacrament may be performed some time after the first birthday. Ashwalayana, on the other hand, insists that Chaulam is to be done in the third year. The Ashwalayana Grihya Sutra further recommends

'that the sacrament should be performed when the Sun has resumed its northerly course. On the day of the ritual a Homa should be performed and offerings of ghee and wood fuel made to Agni (God of Fire). Four earthenware pots filled with rice, barley, pulses and sesamum should be placed near the sacred fire. These are given to the barber as payment with some cash. After the Homa the child should be led away from the sacred fire and asked to sit in front of the barber. The father should sit behind the child, to give moral support.'

The Sutra text mentions the use of a razor, which suggests that the head is to be shaved completely.

The physician Charaka (about 180CE) in his medical text says:

'The trimming of nails, the cutting of hair and the shaving of the head promotes cleanliness, good health and long life. Periodic shaving of the head keeps the scalp free of infection and encourages strong growth of hair.'

The ritual is experienced mainly by boys in devout Brahmin families, but in some parts of India very young girls also experience Chaulam. In modern practice very few young boys have their heads shaved; most people follow the European fashion. The child has a bath after the haircut and enjoys some special sweet dish at lunch.

NEW WORD

Chaulam a child's first haircut

THINGS TO DO

1 Talk to some old people to discover what family customs relating to babies they can remember. You may be able to find out other things from books on folklore.

2 List customs in your family, such as christenings or naming ceremonies.

FOR DISCUSSION

1 Discuss what some of the customs you listed mean.

2 Why are some of these customs less popular than they were?

3 How does a Hindu baby's first outing make him or her aware of the outside world?

19 Scriptures in regional languages (1)

This unit tells you when and why many religious poets re-told earlier Sanskrit works in their regional Indian languages.

Many religious poets in different parts of India composed poetry in regional languages to bring the teachings of earlier Sanskrit works from the Upanishads, the Bhagavata Purana and the Bhagavad-Gita within the reach of ordinary men and women. Jnanadeva lived in Maharashtra and wrote a long **Marathi** poem of 9000 verses in 1290CE, to explain the teachings of the Bhagavad-Gita. In the 16th century, Eknath wrote his Bhagavata in Marathi in order to explain the Bhagavata Purana to ordinary people in their own language. Ramadasa lived in Maharashtra in the 17th century. His Marathi book, the Dasabodha, is influenced by the teachings of the Bhagavad-Gita.

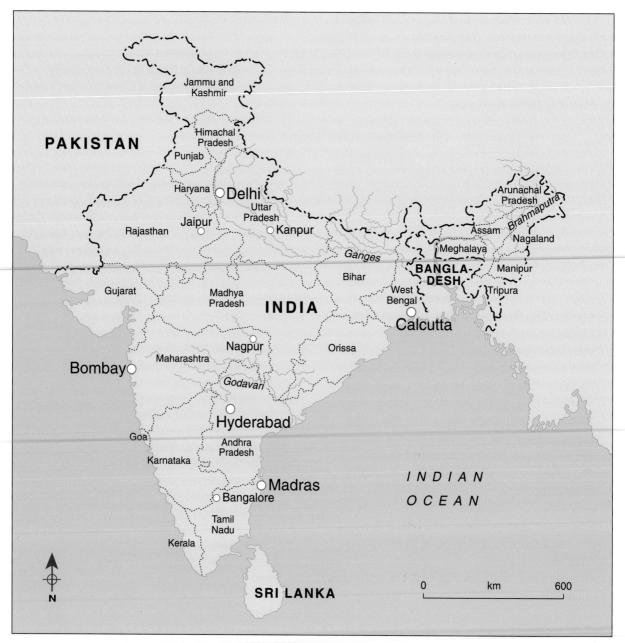

The states of India.

Here are some of Jnanadeva's words:

> 'The soul is different from the body.
>
> The body is affected by consequences of actions.
>
> The plant of ignorance can be uprooted only by wisdom.
>
> A man of action is like the sun, doing his duty selflessly.
>
> Devotion to God ends all sin and social status becomes meaningless.
>
> God accepts any humble offering from a true devotee.'

The popularity of the Rama story

Other religious writers based their works in regional languages on the original Rama story, which is in Sanskrit. Eknath and Ramadasa both wrote their versions in Marathi to promote the worship of God Rama among people who did not know Sanskrit. In the ninth century the poet Kamban wrote a version of the story in **Tamil**, a south Indian language. A **Gujarati** translation of the Ramayana is popular. The poet Krittivasa translated the Ramayana from Sanskrit into **Bengali**; it is a very popular book in Bengal.

Tulsidas (16th century) lived in Uttar Pradesh, in north India. He wrote his **Hindi** version, called Rama-Charita-Manasa (The Lake of Rama's Deeds), in order to bring the teachings of earlier Sanskrit works to ordinary people. In the opening verse he says:

> 'I have written these verses in the local language (Hindi) to tell the Rama story. I have included the teachings of the Puranas and the Vedas in it. I have written the story from the Sanskrit Ramayana by Valmiki.'

All these religious writers felt that Hindu scriptures written in Sanskrit were keeping ordinary people away from the religious tradition. Sanskrit was used for religious writings for many centuries and the orthodox priests were not prepared to accept the scriptures written in regional languages. In spite of such opposition, writers such as Jnanadeva and Tulsidas produced their works in languages which people could understand. These writings in Hindi, Marathi, Bengali, Gujarati and Tamil are still popular today and continue the earlier religious tradition. For that reason they have the same authority as the Sanskrit scriptures in Hinduism.

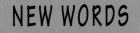

NEW WORDS

Bengali, Gujarati, Hindi, Marathi, Tamil some of the fifteen official Indian languages

FOR DISCUSSION

1 Why did some Hindus think it was important for people to be able to read or listen to the story of Rama in their own language?

2 Why do you think the story of Rama is so popular among Hindus?

THINGS TO DO

1 On your map of India add in the various areas the names of the writers and languages mentioned in this unit.

2 On a sheet of paper draw a vertical line 5cm from the left edge of the page. Write 1200CE at the top and 1700CE at the bottom. Mark a scale of 4cm for each 100 years. On the left side of this line list the writers mentioned in this unit. On the right, list the books they wrote. Leave some space to add some information about the books from Units 20 and 21. You may do this in rough for now.

20 Scriptures in regional languages (2)

This unit tells you how scriptures in regional languages promoted devotion to God. It also describes how manuscripts were prepared.

Hindu poets

Some religious poets who wrote in regional languages not only included the teachings of earlier Sanskrit scripture in their poetry but also promoted **Bhakti**, the devotional way of worshipping God. The practice of Bhakti requires a strong belief in a personal god of love and mercy. The worshipper delights in praising God, remembers God at all times and offers his or her life to the will of God.

Tukaram, a poet living in Maharashtra in the 17th century CE, wrote over 4000 hymns in Marathi stressing complete surrender to and limitless love for God. Here is one of his hymns. Vithoba and Keshava are names for Vishnu.

'May my speech repeat the sweet name of Vithoba.

May my eyes gaze joyfully on his divine face.

May my ears hear of his divine qualities.

Fly, O mind, and rest at the feet of Vithoba.

Hark, O soul, says Tuka, do not forsake Keshava'

Namadeva (14th century CE) wrote many songs in Marathi and stressed that social status was no barrier to following the way of Bhakti towards God.

Surdas (16th century CE) was a blind poet who lived at Agra, in north India. His Hindi verses describe Radha's devotion to God Krishna.

Mirabai (late 15th century CE) wrote devotional songs in Hindi, Braj Bhasha (a form of Hindi) and Gujarati. She was a princess and her devotion to God Krishna is seen in her many songs.

Here is one of them:

'You are my only refuge, O Krishna, the supporter of Mount Govardhana. Your crown of peacock feathers and your saffron-coloured garments are beautiful; your earrings have a unique splendour. Princess Draupadi stands helpless in full assembly. Protect her honour, O Murari. Mira's Lord Giridhara is indeed clever; his lotus-like feet are worthy of worship.'

The poet Kabir was a weaver by trade. He lived in the 15th century CE near Banaras. Orthodox priests persecuted him because he challenged their authority. He wrote devotional songs in Hindi, and maintained that Vishnu, Rama, Krishna and Allah were all names of the One Supreme God, who was neither in mosque nor in images. He preached devotion to God as a way of finding spiritual freedom.

Manuscripts

The Indian climate easily damages manuscript material. Animal skin (parchment) was considered 'impure' material for sacred writings, so in north India birch bark and birch leaves were used for recording sacred texts, and in the south, palm leaves were used. Paper was introduced into India in about 800CE but it was not used for sacred manuscripts until 1290CE.

Before the texts were written down on birch, the inner bark of the birch was cut into smooth pieces, which were fastened together with a cord. Reed pens and black ink were used for writing.

If palm was being used, the leaves were boiled, dried and flattened. A small hole was cut in each leaf so that the leaves could be held together in layers with a cord threaded through the holes. A pointed iron pencil was used to scratch the letters on palm leaves and soot or lamp-black was rubbed into the grooves.

The use of printing for sacred texts began in 1849CE. The Rig-Veda was printed in Sanskrit between 1849 and 1874. The Manava Kalpa Sutra in Sanskrit was printed in London in 1861. In the same year Kamban's Ramayana in Tamil was printed in

This palm leaf manuscript shows some verses from the Bhagavata Purana. This text stresses the importance of Bhakti, devotion to God.

Madras, India. Now sacred texts in all major Indian languages and scripts are available in printed books.

NEW WORD

Bhakti a way of worshipping a god or goddess by complete surrender to his or her will

FOR DISCUSSION

1 Would printing or learning about God in regional languages help Hindus to learn more about their religion?

2 Murti has often been mentioned in this book. Check that you know what the word means. Discuss which is the best English word to translate it. Is any translation really satisfactory?

THINGS TO DO

1 Add the writers and books mentioned in this unit to the time chart begun in Unit 19.

2 Mark the places mentioned in this unit on your map of India.

21 Law books

This unit is about the scriptures known as law books, which give the social and religious duties of the four traditional social groups in Hindu society.

Hindu law

All people have certain duties, depending on the job they do. Some duties are imposed by law, while others are optional, although there is a moral force behind them. For example, a nurse has a duty to provide medical care for the patient. A doctor has a duty to prescribe the correct treatment for the illness, yet the treatment must not be illegal. A lorry driver has a duty to obey all the traffic laws and to maintain the lorry in good condition, and must not carry any illegal goods. Nowadays, these laws are laid down by a body such as Parliament and people must follow them.

A long time ago, in traditional Hindu society, the duties of the four varnas (social groups) were laid down in scriptures called the Dharmashastra, ancient law books written in Sanskrit and recommending the religious and social duties of the people. These codes of behaviour had the force of law at first.

A bridegroom holds his bride's hand as she is given in marriage by her father.

Although they were based on laws believed to come from God, they were modified as time went on to suit the changing needs of society.

The code of Manu has 2685 verses and probably dates from 300CE. Manu says that right and wrong can be decided through the Vedas, traditional practice, good conduct of the righteous and a person's conscience. The code of Yajnavalkya probably dates from 500CE. It, too, deals with dharma (religious and social duty) but stresses the legal aspect of social duties. These two codes largely formed the basis of Hindu law.

Hindu law is a personal law and applies to Hindus. It relates to adoption, marriage and divorce, and joint family properties. The laws passed by the Indian Parliament have reduced the importance of the ancient law books. Some rules from them are still useful, mainly those dealing with marriage and varna duties.

Here are some rules from the ancient law books:

Giving a girl in marriage

'A father, a grandfather, a brother or a male from the same family can give away a bride. If the seniormost male dies then the younger one in order can perform the ritual, provided he is of sound mind.'   (Yajnavalkya 1.63.)

Duties of Kshatriyas, Vaishyas and Shudras

'A Kshatriya's first duty is to protect people and property. Agriculture, banking, commerce and dairy-farming are suitable occupations for a Vaishya. Serving the three twice-born varnas is the duty of a Shudra. If a Shudra cannot get a good living by service, he may become a tradesman or learn a craft, but he should always serve the upper varnas.'
(Yajnavalkya 1.119–21.)

Importance of varna in marriage

'For the first marriage a bride from the same varna is recommended.'   (Manu 3.12.)

Duties of a Brahmin householder

'A Brahmin should earn a living and maintain his family by an occupation which does not affect other men's interest.

'A Brahmin's speech and feelings must befit his birth, wealth, age and education.

'No guest should be allowed to stay in a Brahmin's house without receiving hospitality, food, water and bed.

'He must not restrain a cow from drinking water or suckling her calf, if he sees her in those acts.'   (Manu 4.2, 18, 29, 59.)

Status of Women

'Women must be honoured and given clothes and ornaments by their fathers, brothers, husbands and brothers-in-law to promote (their own) good fortune.

'Where women are honoured, there the Gods shower blessings; but where they are ill treated, sacred rites bring no rewards.'
(Manu: 5.55–56.)

FOR DISCUSSION

1 Why do the scriptures deal with behaviour as well as teachings about God?

2 Why do Hindus consider it better to do your own dharma badly than to do the dharma of another caste well?

THINGS TO DO

1 Add names and books listed in this unit to your time line. Make a neat copy of it in your notebook.

22 Hindu funerals

This unit shows how the Sutra texts describe the detailed performance of rituals, for example funerals.

We have already seen that the naming ceremony, the sacred thread ritual and weddings are carried out according to customs laid down in special books. It will not be too surprising to find that the way a funeral should be conducted is also set out in the Grihya Sutra of Ashwalayana.

Cremation

Cremation is the normal practice at Hindu funerals, but very young babies and **Sannyasins** (those who have given up all worldly ties) are buried. An ancient text gives a detailed description of a Hindu cremation:

'The corpse should be bathed by men if it is male, by women if it is female, and it should be dressed in new clothes. It is placed on a stretcher made of bamboo and carried to the cremation ground near a local river. The nearest male relative walks in front carrying some live coals in an earthenware pot. Slow-burning logs are used to build the pyre. Those who can afford it add a few sticks of sandalwood. The body is placed on the pyre with its head pointing to the north. The eldest or the youngest son of the deceased walks three times round the pyre with a lighted torch, then ignites the pyre at the four corners. When the pyre is burning strongly, he puts five spoonfuls of ghee onto the pyre as offerings to Agni, **Soma**, this world, Earth and the other world. The funerary priest chants mantras as the offerings of ghee are made. When the skull cracks through the action of heat, the atman is believed to escape into the atmosphere. Walking round the pyre with a lighted torch prevents the soul from escaping back to Earth and becoming a ghost to haunt the living.'

(Ashwalayana Grihya Sutra.)

A corpse is taken to the cremation ground.

A pyre is lighted to cremate the corpse.

The soul's destiny

Hindus believe that atman, the soul, never dies, but continues to exist in different bodies in successive lives. The body in the next life is determined by the consequences of actions in an earlier life.

Here is a verse from the oldest scripture, the Rig-Veda, addressed to the corpse as the funeral pyre is ignited:

> 'May your sight be absorbed into the sun and your atman escape into the atmosphere. May your atman reach the region of light or once more return to Earth, or perhaps go to the waters or to the plants, taking on new bodies, depending on the consequences of its actions.'   (Rig-Veda 10.16.3.)

At the end of its long cycle of rebirths, the soul achieves its spiritual freedom and reaches Brahman.

NEW WORDS

Sannyasin a man who has given up all possessions and worldly ties to devote his life to God

Soma a sacred plant formerly used in Vedic ritual but now extinct

A Hindu funeral in Britain

In Britain a Hindu corpse is placed in a coffin and cremated. Religious rituals, such as walking round the corpse, are carried out at the funeral parlour. An incense stick is used instead of a lighted torch and, to console the mourners, verses from the Bhagavad-Gita are read in the chapel at the crematorium.

FOR DISCUSSION

1 What are the arguments for and against

  a the rebirth of the soul?

  b the idea that the soul is only born once?

  c the idea that there is no soul and therefore nothing to survive death?

2 Which arguments for rebirth are a Hindu likely to find most convincing?

THINGS TO DO

1 Check that your map of India is complete, then make a neat copy for your notebook.

Glossary

Arati a ritual performed with a ghee lamp and ignited camphor

Artha earning money

Atman the individual soul

Aum the Sacred Syllable of Hinduism, a word for God

Avatar God's appearance on Earth to protect the good and punish and destroy the evil. An incarnation

Bhajan a devotional hymn sung as a chorus with music

Bhakti a way of worshipping a god or goddess by complete surrender to his or her will

Brahman the Supreme Spirit of Hinduism

Chaulam a child's first haircut

Dasara the day after Navaratri

Deity a god or goddess

Dharma social and religious duty of a person according to his or her varna (social group), stage in life and occupation

Dhyana deep meditation

Gayatri verse the widely used prayer from the Rig-Veda, praising the Sun God

Ghee clarified butter

Guru a teacher who guides his followers on spiritual and religious questions

Homa a ritual in which offerings of wood, ghee and grain are made to Agni (God of Fire)

Kama enjoying the good things of life

Karma the consequences of action; also action or work

Krishna God Vishnu's eighth and most important avatar

Mantra a sacred phrase from scriptures

Moksha spiritual freedom of the soul

Murti or rupa an image of a god or goddess used in worship. It can be human, animal, plant or bird, or a combination of these

Namaskara a greeting made by putting the palms of the hands together and bowing

Oral tradition the way early Hindus passed on sacred texts by word of mouth to the next generation

Pandit a Hindu priest; a learned man

Prasad blessed offering

Puja the most common form of worship

Puranas ancient texts containing Hindu mythology

Purusha-Sukta a hymn describing the sacrifice of Primal Man

Rig-Veda the oldest Hindu scripture

Samskara sacrament; a life-cycle ritual such as a baby's naming ceremony, the sacred thread ceremony, marriage or cremation

Sannyasin a man who has given up all possessions and worldly ties to devote his life to God

Sanskrit an ancient language of India. Many Hindu scriptures are written in Sanskrit

Shruti scriptures 'revealed' by God and 'heard' by sages

Smriti scriptures based on 'remembered tradition'

Soma a sacred plant formerly used in Vedic ritual but now extinct

Upanayana the sacred thread ceremony

Varna a social group. The four traditional varnas in Hindu society are Brahmin (priests, professionals), Kshatriya (administrators, soldiers), Vaishya (business people) and Shudra (farm labourers, artisans)

Yoga a system of philosophy which combines control of the mind and physical exercises to achieve freedom of the soul. It is also used simply to mean meditation